A Poet's Ebb

And Flow

By Dudley (CHRIS) Christian

A

Pause For Poetry ©

Publication

Acknowledgement:

Special thanks to my wife, Marilyn Christian for compiling, organizing and finalizing the books of my collections. Her photographing and editing skills were vital to all of my works.

ISBN: 978-0-9877501-5-0

First Edition April 2012
Revised Edition June 2017

Cover Photographs © Marilyn Christian:

Front Cover: Just another Caribbean cruise dock
Back Cover: Oregon Coast

<u>An Opening Word by the Author...</u>

Many people often ask:

"How do you write and do you have to often rewrite your material?"

I have long summed up my answer to the above with the following:

"A Word, the written word, small purveyor of a thought, so like a thought, once thought, cannot be recalled, so too, a word once writ, should need NOT be re-written, for with such licence, we would but change ... the very substance of the thought."

... DNC © 1970

Dudley (Chris) Christian founded and hosted the first and only "PAUSE FOR POETRY" show dedicated solely to the introduction of new and unknown poets and their works. This TV series ran from 1974 to 1985.

Table of Contents

Tides Ebb And Flow...1

Here We Sit Talking 2

Beautiful Persistent Sunworshipper 6

While I'm Writing To You Dear..............................8

My Prayers Are Answered......................................8

As A Woman...9

Only A Picture 10

Brighten Some Corner 11

Beautiful Eyes So Softly 12

I Was Just A Blackbird 13

There Are But Two People...................................14

Oh So Dark And Dismal Grey..............................16

The Weatherman Today Says Rain.......................18

I Saw The Big Big Fair City...............................20

My Colours They Have Always Been....................21

Gee But It's Calm And Peaceful 23

A Bright And Sunny Day 24

You Cold White Soft Demon 25

Old Seven Mile Stretch......................................27

Silver Dollars All Aglitter...................................29

Let Me Sail All My Days Away............................30

Alas Darling I'm Only A Dreamer 31

'Twas The Night Before Full Moon...........................32

Just Like Liquid Glass It Lies................................34

Spotted Jagged Treed Or Bare................................36

'Tis But A Tiny Bit Of Weed..................................38

Do Not Bite Your Lovely Finger 40

Bluer Than The Heavenly Sky.................................42

A Wisp Of A Dream..44

Worshipping Your Idols.......................................45

Tak Me Hom Too De Wam Breeze..........................46

I'm Just A Lonely Drifter 49

Just Call To Me My Darling...................................50

I'm Asking Your Forgiveness.................................52

Today I Cried For You..53

Blue Blue Blue 54

I Believe In Christmas 56

So This Is Christmas... Is It? 57

Late Tonight...63

It's Been Nice...64

Heaven Earth and Tearful Heart............................65

Table of Contents Poem 66

Dear Reader:

As the end of day rolls on, we often sit and think of the Beauty of this great World of ours. We also think of another day, week, month or year that has passed us by.

It is, at such moments, that I hope to offer you some insight, which will help carry you through life's turmoils. So go ahead now, imagine yourself back a day, or three, as you sat on some beach or river's bank, or the restful tranquility of a silent and reflective lake-front.

Take a good look, or journey through your memories, and as you do, recall your memories makers which gave you cause to compare, even as these few words of mine give you reason to live them again, as you at least break into a smile, or a warm glow... Feels great, doesn't it ???

Strange, one could almost take this table of contents and read them as a poem of itself (see page 66). That is because the whole World is made with, from and of, POETRY… Thanks for trying mine…

If I can offer you this, then my words here will have been successfully composed and I too shall be Happy...

So thank you, my unknown, or even well known, reader. I am most appreciative that you have taken your precious time to see a little of what makes my life a part of yours with each so unique tho so entwined... Again, Thank You...

Tides Ebb and Flow

Here in a crag of rock sit I
Listening to the waters flow
Like cars in an underground tunnel
Sounds its entering ebb and flow
Splish splash they thump and thud
As a post beam joins the array
To batter the shore ramrod-like
While here in a crag I lay
Apple core matches and shavings
Roots kelp dead fish and seaweed
Leaves moss seagulls slow swimming
Flotsam and jetsam are these
Off like the head of a maiden
With hair long dark brown all aglow
Waves the brown seaweed fast rockbound
Falling on tides ebb and flow
Pile driver so nearby and noisily
Plies in its unending toils
Barriers to erect for a safekeeping
But the tides ebb and flow each one foils
Left back awhile it to nature
Once more to nature it returns...
As the rocks grind to pulp most things
Which the tides ebb and flow carries on

Here We Sit Talking

Here we sit talking on the white sand
Close to the crystal waters of Grand Cayman
A girl from far across the sea
A girl whom fate has brought here to me

Let's take a drive I then to her did say
Up to the caves found on Old Spotts bay
We'll walk across the waters as the coral is rough
And enjoy the light surf of which one can't get enough

Fine with me she says and taking my hand
Invites her relations who also love this dear land
Together we leave for the place cross the waters
This cousin this mother and my love her daughter

We saw a man as we got to the beach
Out in the water his line trying to reach
There were shells on the beach in a galore
Where the natives had brought
Their conch catch ashore

As we walked in the water there we did see
Hundreds of minnows and fishes moving swiftly
Just before reaching where the cave lies
We saw a school of sprats, jacks and goggle eyes

On the beach there was lying quite stiff and still
A bird which someone had been trying to kill
There also was an urchin tho quite harmless I could see
For it had been washed out awhile from the sea

We walked to the cave through the powdery sand
For this beach has the finest in the Island
We had to bend real low to enter the cave
Tho there were some bats all the women were brave

We entered the first room
And for awhile just stood there
Discussing the beauty and the moldy scented air
Then I thought to show to them the rest
Hoping they wouldn't be scared by the other cave pests

We went through the slit which is high tho small
Observed bats hanging by their feet 'long the walls
After inspecting and holding short discussion
We were leaving but saw a rat making an inspection

I picked up a stick to hit it without delay
But it saw me and ran into a hole then away
We left the cave and returned by the water
Were amused by a man with two lines in the water

At first we thought this quite a lark
But he said quite seriously he fished for a shark
Into the car then we did go
Thru the old road I drove the church them to show

It is now quite old with no window panes
There are no doors left and the roof lets in the rain
But down thru the ages its name will be warm
As being the one building
Not destroyed by the '32 storm

We read quite a few of the headstones found there
And it seems that Watler most of them did bear
Then out on the seashore we decided to trod
Where lies that sweet beauty created only by God

Tho rocks were quite sharp no one seemed to mind
But on our return the sprightly one lagged behind
As we came to the shore there again we did find
Quite a few fish which the tide had left behind

But as there was water enough for them in to stay
We left them that the next tide would take them away
Once more we did stop now my favorite picture to see
The beauty of the Sunset reflected across the sea

And many times tho I've seen it before
I'll recall that day with her by my side evermore
Alas back to the hotel we finally went
A bit tired but happy for a lovely day well spent

Then as there on the patio I held her near
I could feel she'd someday return to me here
And as if she could read then clearly my mind
When I kissed her she vowed to forever be mine

So now tho she's gone oh so far away
I live only in hopes of her returning day
I'm sure she will for she knows I love her so
And I know she loves me
That's why she cried when she had to go

So tho here alone even now I must be
Remember that our love just must be
Yes you're the angel which from my rib God created
The one I feel was for me always and only created

Beautiful Persistant Sunworshipper

She came by in Early Springtime

Dropped Winters garb for cool scant Summers wear

And like the Sun her body from flowed warmth

It was Summers ebb and fall

And one could feel the soft cold breath of Winter

Play upon the reaches of her warmth

Her lithe form yet uncovered

Save but for skirt short

And blouse of sleeveless form

Her bronzed skin reflective of her warmth

Upon her head of golden curls

Which fluttered down like feathers light

Upon her waiting shoulders

A net which seemed of spider weave there lay

And summer Sun played its tattoo on her

As upon the beach she resteth still that day

A solar blanket she enveloping Suns warmth

Then Winters long and cold and icy fingers

Reached out awhile 'neath safe shield

Of a passing cloud

To reach and reach deep – deep within her warmth

No move made she the moment for

No thought gave she to stay short the chill she felt

For soon the sun returneth with its warmth

Aye -- but cunningly and cold old Winter waited

Waited for the fall of sun -- the last warmth of day

Then fast returning -- she to capture

When eve had been and gone

When night upon the world did rule supreme

Here Winters touch would be unhindered ---

Yet --- there she lay content she in her warmth

Enjoyment full in mind

Recalling warmth of the late Summer day

Forgetful of the chill which she had felt

Next morn a visitor dismal, dark had she

One who calls but once each life within a trip to take

As there she lay in fevered warmth a-shaking

So lay she in extreme inner warmth now so unwanted

Yet shake the chill of Winters touch

She now no longer could

So as days Sun departed she did follow

To grace perhaps some greater warm surroundings

Or be companion constant to the soft cold Winter wind

Or mayhap wait another Springtime in to return again

While I'm Writing to You Dear

While I'm writing to you dear this letter
And the words they come straight from my heart
Tho they're saying I'll love you forever
You say its best Sweetheart for us to part
I gave you love which you never cared for
I was proud to have you for my wife
But it seems it was wild life that you cared for
Thus you left to live your Honky-tonk life
Oh Sweetheart I hope that you'll be happy
In your search for riches untold
You gave up the love we had completely
Cause you preferred to have silver and gold
Just remember the promises you've broken
And the heart you've filled so full of pain
And recall the solemn vows you've taken
You can never be free to love again

My Prayers Are Answered

My prayers are answered
My dreams come true
I know I don't want anyone but you
For you have given me a love that is true
And no one else no one else can do
We had our quarrels
We've had our strife
But yet I'm glad that you are my wife
And now I'm happy
The rest of my life
Living with you living with you
Just living with you

As a Woman

As a woman
As a woman among men
You turn me on ere once again
You fill my mind with thoughts
Of things I'd dreamed of oft
You thrill my days its true
With just the memory of you
As a Woman
As a Woman
Joy to my life you bring
Cleansing my life my everything
You bubble over like a morning spring
Cascading o'er flowers in the Spring
Rendering full blossom once again
To a heart hardened hard by men
As a Woman
As a Woman
You in my arms I'd take
Even tho the result could me break
Yet for joy or love or freedoms sake
'Tis a chance which any man would take
To ease his mind and remove the ache
Which plays upon my soul for YOU
As a Woman

Only a Picture

Only a picture pressed to my heart
Only a memory of you
You'll live all your life
As some other man's wife
But I will always love you
You'll never know how you hurt me
I'd never thought one could be so mean
Yet I'll never hold it against you
For one time you gave love to me
You just can't believe or know dear
The way in which my love for you grows
You can't understand this feeling
'Cause your closed heart blinded your love
One day tho in only a picture
Your memory will fade away
But my love for you will continue
As long as on God's earth I stay
So dearest Sweetheart my only Darling
As again to my heart you I do press
This picture my only memento
With love seeking hands you I caress
Yet you're only a picture in plastic
So warm, so protected so secure
But to me you'll be a lifelong memory
And there's no one who your memory can remove
Only a picture pressed to my heart
Only a memory of you
Only the one you loved at the start
Only so in love with you

Brighten Some Corner

Brighten some corner in this world so dim
Make someone happy being there with him
Show some little girl the way to travel right
Help some lost stranger in the dark cold night
Spread a little sunshine as you go along
Bring a little happiness with a word or song
Tell the age old story of God and love and life
Be the one forever to stay the start of strife
Walk softly as you go upon your way
Lend a helping hand to someone everyday
Your life will be happier filled with sunshine
Brighten some corner in this world of mine
Take my hand and lead me to the pastures green
Show my weary eyes things they haven't seen
Let my heart rejoice in the knowledge of your love
Let my heart be always fulfilled as it is now
Then when time is over and life has run out
When we face eternity we'll know what its about
For truly then we'll be together for all time
For in life in death in heaven you will still be mine
Help someone find peace here on this world below
Tho it be not me I'll happy be if this you find I know
And fondly I'll forever in my memories recall
You spread sunshine in my life when I was losing all
You'll be repaid in measure full by the God above
By joy and happiness full store and a true eternal love

Beautiful Eyes So Softly

Beautiful eyes so softly
Shining with love divine
Bringing to me a fond memory
Of days before you were mine
Face that's all aglitter bright
With smiles of happy dreams
Waiting our chance to make so right
Our beautiful hopes and dreams
Then came the day we'd hoped for
When at last you would be mine
You'd come to me and always be
The only love I'd hoped to find
But fate seemed against us Darling
On that beautiful sunshine day
And life to me seemed so unfair
When death took you away
You lay there in your splendour
So like in dreams I'd held of you
But in this dream you'll stay forever
Its my last long look at you
Still in memories you will always
Smile with big shining eyes my dear
And I'll live alone now you're gone
In dreams of those beautiful days

I Was Just a Blackbird

I was just a blackbird flying all around
Being a pest to all the poor men in town
I'd destroy their yellow corn
When it was old enough to cut
I'd dig their beans from out the ground everyday but
Ah yes it is amusing the way the world now stands
With liars thieves war and criminals around
You see a human shot a dove
Right where I now stand
I saw its pure plumage upon this dirty ground
It brought me to my better mind
I saw all men were killing right
Leaving sin and trouble like me around
While the pure was removed and hidden deep from sight
I knew I couldn't be like the Dove I had seen quite dead
But I dressed for that revival and was glad that I went
For I know now I've a chance
For a pure feather in my head
For I received the message of love
Which the dead Dove sent
He only asked that I would try
Would try to mend my ways
He said the Lord still wanted me to fly around up there
No matter what my colour was
If I'm good til my last days
He'll make my feathers oh so pure
And take me home up there

There Are But Two People

There are but two people in this world

They are strange enough

A boy and a girl

With but one reason

To live or to die

Strange that those people

Are just — You and I

You are the person

Who fills all my dreams

The ultimate reasons for all of my schemes

The passion

The anger

The grief or the warmth

Which I feel rushing onwards

Or just creeping along

You are the echo to my every song

The bit of my life that never moves on

The vision of heaven I see everyday

My moon

Sun

Stars that shine on my way

Yes — you are the one that just must be

Cause without you there never could be a me

I am the person

Opposite you

That tries to fulfill each wish for you

That lives

As you want

Far or nearby

That smiles

Or frowns

Listens or cries

The person who takes your hand

In distress

Who's always nearby

With tender caress

The first and the last

And all of the others

Your father, your brother

Your friend

Son or lover

Yet — yes it is real strange

That we two even exist

<u>Oh So Dark and Dismal Grey</u>

Oh so dark and dismal grey

Are the clouds that hang around

As the darker night enshrouds

The hill the vale the town

The waters all icy calm

Appears so dark and empty too

In colourless death they lay

So dark and distant in hue

But look there comes the sun

In its morning Glory bright

Spreading its new red gold upon

Each place that sees its light

It has a painted gold red carpet

Upon the waters shimmering blue

Crested with gold, silver, diamonds

Each droplet of mornings dew

The green of the hillsides all sparkle

As the red drops of the gold tips the blades

The snow on the hilltop's a marvel

As the Sun touches valleys and dales

Now the dark clouds have all silver linings

And the world is not dismal and grey

Each nook and cranny is shining

As the Sun opens bright a new day

Oh we're so glad to see you returning

To remove the dark tidings we knew

While the dark night had us feeling

That we'd lost sight Sun ever of you

So travel your Journeys e'er over

Until your short visit is done

Tho we'll feel down as dark settles over

We'll await your new rising Oh Sun

The Weatherman Today Says Rain

The weatherman today says rain

But he is wrong once again

Yesterday he was telling you

'Twould be so bright and sunny too

The Sun gets up the sky to light

God's day to start again so right

But man has changed to suit his pay

The time of times God's scheduled day

The clock we find no longer gives

Corrective time to suit God's will

Our days grow short and harder too

And we're to blame yes me and you

Had God wanted his hours cut off

He'd have fashioned day another way

And had God not sought to please us oft

Mankind would not exist today

Yet man has said that God is dead

For reasons financial now instead

For man will not to God time give

If that time may mean another dollar bill

If man believed there's yet a Master

To whom he'd have to pay hereafter

He'd have to pay that God His due

In time and monies lost its true

So easier yet for man instead

To build up Gold saying "God is dead"

Than build treasures in Heaven above

And learn true friendship -- joy and love

So the weatherman today said rain

But he is wrong once more again

I Saw the Big Big Fair City

Much like the snow which froze upon the hill

I saw the evening sun set, I heard the whippoorwill

But thru it all my heart grew colder still

For this city is my prison, my hell and yet my home

Cause of my own choice I did to here come

It took my life, my name, my joys and all that I adored

So cold cold city that's why I hate you now

I hate you for your beauty so artificial and so false

I hate you for your prisons and your bar

I hate you for your long green

That blinds my very thoughts

And for the Godless creature that you are

You've built on bones of people

Which you have massacred

Your living is on exploitation of the poor

Your rich you defend with your legal counterparts

Whilst your greedy taxes just grab more and more

Too late to try to change the way you live big city

Cause your feet are too long buried in your mire

Your corrupt mind is now but a thing to pity

But your just rewards are waiting in Hell's fire

My Colours They Have Always Been

My colours they have always been

Since I can first recall

The things which please my memories

With sparkling wonders all

So when I chance to gaze again

On hues or shades I love

I chance to recall ages past

When you were here my love

The gold of nature's sunshine

The gold of Autumn leaves

The gold of soft bird feathers

The gold of mountain streams

These fill me with enticement

As Earth's beauty they do bare

Like you fill me with excitement

As I stroke your golden hair

Then there's another colour

Which thrills my daily life

It gives me lasting pleasure

In the world so full of strife

It's the blue of Heaven paintings

It's the blue of oceans calm

The blue of bluebirds singing

And the blue of fires warm

Yet tho these blues bring beauty

As to my life they always do

Your blue eyes bring contentment full

Each time I look at you

And thus my colours linger

Alive and warm to me

The golds and blues I ponder

Each time their hues I see

But of all my passing fancies

Whereon these colours dwell

They look their best upon you dear

And I'm sure they always will

Gee But It's Calm and Peaceful

Gee but its calm and peaceful

For four in the afternoon

The sea its like a painted dream

O'er shadowed by the moon

The seagulls are softly gliding

On the sweet smelling salty air

While snow on the mountains is falling

And God's peace is everywhere

The sun 'tis lightly covered

Removing some of its brightness and heat

The clouds have lazily drifted

In a thousand pictures beneath

The painter of nature is busy

With his array of colours for fall

But the silence is deep and sleepy

As God's peace falls over all

No noise of cities or engines

No guns or motors doth break

The peaceful serenity of nature

When nature her deep sleep doth take

For to the ears of the blinded person

Or the eyes of those whose hearing is gone

There echoes and appears ever God's Son

While God's Peace reigns over all

A Bright and Sunny Day

A bright and sunny day
With cool crisp wintry air
A thousand birds at play
A-flying everywhere
The boats by dozens float
So near the mountain side
There in the cove they float
Protected from the tide
The rods and lines aglitter
Happy faces all agleam
The sounds of joyous twitter
From every boat doth stream
Big boats now and small boats
And boats of colours varied
Boats with oars and boats with sails
And boats by engines powered
They sit there in the Sun and laze
Their minds afar their thoughts ablaze
With earthly wealth and gain
They think not for the day that be
They care not for its keeping
Respectless of the one who gave
It, for His reverence keeping
And yet our Lord He loves them all
Blessing them with catches grand
As He keeps the fog far out at sea
While smiling on ungrateful man

You Cold White Soft Demon

You cold white soft demon

Which to some men bring joy

Your coat of cold you throw upon

Those places where you can employ

Peoples, to live and work in you

Spending their nights and their days

In awe, fearsome that somehow

You'll in your grasp them get one day

Yet many rejoice to see you

As you in such splendour descend

To blanket around and cause havoc

To the hard working and moving men

But alas like much evils you too pass

And on your cold path you go

Seeking other enjoyment by giving

Cooling Winter wherever you go

Yet without your kiss 'twould be funny

To see the seasons all change

You're needed I guess to help nature

Balance the heat wind and rain

Your first breath to us such splendour

As the multicolours of fall

While your parting breath releases to us

Tiny flowers bees and birds singing all

That's followed by Summer to warm us

And let us enjoy full earths store

And give us a time to prepare again

For your cold wintry kisses once more

Oh snow of Winter you awe me

With your beauty and cold which I dread

I hope tho that you'll always come faithfully

For without your kiss earth would be dead

Old Seven Mile Stretch

Old seven mile stretch as it is called

Is quite renown and beloved by all

It holds upon it our clubs, hotels, cottages fair

As it accepts with a smile the cool sea air

It whispers to the waves which beside it roll

It covers millions in old Spanish silver and gold

There are spots upon it which should be dark red

To remind us of pirates and slaves

Who once upon it lay dead

Again there are songs sung 'neath the weeping willow

By the lovers which are sheltered in its cool shadow

Other spots there be more popular still

Which is couple crowded for a moonlight thrill

Far far away one can hear yet the band

As calypso songs linger along the white sands

There the beach parties still thrill visitors about

Lets go to old seven mile still is the shout

Some people have tried it to rename

With fancy and long and beautiful names

Yet all they have tried have all been in vain

For seven mile stretch it remains just the same

It gets in your hair your shoes and your eyes

Tho it's tempting to all, it's clean you soon realize

The warmth of it is more pleasing still

Than the warmth of any liquor

Which has passed from a still

Throughout the world I've searched far and near

Yet purer and whiter no beach can compare

Yet I feel that it all soon from us will go

To people from afar who love to be on it so

Old Seven Mile stretch how I wish you were mine

I never would part with your white sands so fine

And long long ere my days have gone on their way

My young would enjoy the Sunset

The Moonlight

And YOU Old Seven Mile Bay

Silver Dollars All Aglitter

Silver dollars all aglitter

As you shine on on your way

So glad are we to see again

Oh Sun your face today

You warm the icy waters

And our hearts as you pass by

You brighten our darkest corners

When you smile there in the sky

The gulls over the water linger

In ecstasy I'm sure

For the warmth you afford them

They'll be grateful evermore

Why Sun e'en your mortal enemy

The clouds which hide your face

Are so glad your light to see

That they scurry everyplace

The ships and boats move softly

On the waters lest they stir

That blanket of your silver bright

Or your soft painting mar

The water is so quiet calm

And seems so well relaxed

I'm sure oh Sun like me they're glad

Your warm touch to welcome back

Let Me Sail All My Days Away

Let me sail all my days away
O'er oceans of blue, gold, or silver
O'er seas and rivers so endless
O'er tales of sorrows untold
Let me sail ere my life is over
Let my mind and heart be at rest
Let my life while I live it
Be filled with enjoyment
And here after death let me rest
Let my body pass into yonder
On the crest of some foaming wave
And in stormy or silent sea I'll lie there
Content in my salt water grave
Let me sail fore my short life is over
Onwards to the setting of Sun
Let my days and nights intermingle
'Til my mornings and night times are one
Let my heart feel content and repentant
Let my body keep warm and alive
Less I forget the peace of fulfillment
Which from these Oceans I derive
Too long tho it seemeth at daybreak
'Tis but a short time until the dusk
Fill my day with joy and forgiving
Let me ever in thee place my trust
Let me sail all my days away
O'er oceans, 'cross mountains and bay
O'er peoples like me happy to be
Ever sailing our first love the Sea

Alas Darling I'm Only a Dreamer

The sunlight is falling
To brighten the land and the sea
And it brings back warm memories
Of when you were here with me
To touch it would bring me pleasure
To capture it to you it I'd give
That your heart and life forever
Would be warmed as long as you live
No Winter or cold night would haunt you
No sorrow or love that's gone cold
If I could capture the Sunshine
I'd make it forever your own
I'd take you to nightless places
Put sunbeams as a crown on your head
Weave a dress of sunbeams for you
And on a Rainbow I'd fashion your bed
You'd shine far brighter than morning
When a cloudless noontime is near
And your eyes like the blue of the heavens
Would be large, love-filled and clear
Oh, but alas Darling I'm only a dreamer
Who must live on the dreams that I build
Yet I love you tho I'm but a dreamer
Still love you forever I will
So take my hand gentle Darling
And bid not to me a farewell
Come again sit here in my dwelling
Bring your warmth here where I dwell

'Twas the Night Before Full Moon

'Twas the night before Full moon

And far across the sea

Came the brightest softest moonbeams

One did ever see

They shone so soft and sweetly

That I just could have died

To know you were so far away

From my sinful side

I'd never realized before the love

Which true beauty shows

I'd never felt so down and out

As I gazed and asked what it was all about

'Cause I never knew you were so near

Both close at home and way out here

I thought you'd tread on solid sod

I said a ship can have no God

I'm sorry and I beg forgiveness

For I should have known you in the stillness

I just worked and sinned all day

And at night felt ashamed to pray

I'd never thought much of life

Just fickle fun which ended in strife

Then one day on a snow laden bow

I chanced to see what I see now

Yes you were there in the Moon and snow

While death loomed on the ship so low

The snow was pure and oh so white

The ship was dark it held no light

Yet there as far as one could see

The love of Yours and sins of me

'Cause the moon will full tomorrow night

But I'm glad that you're by my side tonight

So Lord I'd like to give you thanks

And ask you to forgive my pranks

For now I've found a girl that I can love

As long as You are up above

It was you God who wasn't by my side

Not this poor little blue-eyed child

Yet I know now you are always near

To watch us too with loving care

That one day we too heaven shall share

Just Like Liquid Glass It Lies

Just like liquid glass it lies

Reflecting soft sky's shades of blue

Responding to the winds that tries

To frost and etch its glassy hue

Soon the wind must pass it knows

And its glassy hue return

While the Suns rays paintings throw

To repaint o'er every rippled one

Now five, six, seven now ten

Softly on its surface rests

Birds that flew overhead when

The ship did o'er it cause wave crests

Alas the ship has now gone on

And these birds rippleless glide

Watching portrayed as they bow down

Their plumage as they wash with pride

Red webbed feet that swim beneath

Black tipped beak that seek for food

White or grey crest breast so neat

Gliding o'er crystal waters smooth

Bits of logs flotsam and drift

Tiny ripples from tiny fish

Cigarette butts and such they lift

Seeking for a tasty dish

Joined now by on floating log

Two crows shiny black as jet

Nibbling at worms in the log

Or dropped food fast they try to get

Still again in glass-like haze

Birds and boats and lands and tree

Mirrored are they all who gaze

At calm and still majestic Sea

Spotted Jagged Treed or Bare

Spotted jagged treed or bare

Sloping rising flat or round

Filled to full with space to spare

Rocky sandy muddy ground

Green and live and growing still

Dead and grey and dying yet

Look o'er at the lonely hill

Each scene that you seek you'll get

Tho the splendour all still lives

Tho the insects small still crawl

Tho the songbird sweetly gives

Music in each chirp and call

Feel the breeze from o'er the sea

Feel the warmth of Summers Sun

Feel the life in shrub and tree

As the flowers open one by one

Then behold down by the feet

Many boats there lazy float

Waiting to relive the treat

In solemn tranquility they float

Man has come to look around

Man has come to here enjoy

In his selfishness he's found

Only ways to beauty destroy

Still tho all of natures touched

Still tho time has been and passed

Beauty yet it seems untouched

As it blooms like in the past

Hill of beauty and delight

You in colour blazed lives on

With rainbows hues both day and night

Caressed by soft breeze and birds song

'Tis But a Tiny Bit of Weed

'Tis but a tiny bit of weed

Which some machine has pressed

Covered o'er with paper thin

Which between lips you caress

'Tis but a tiny bit of tar

Mixed with nicotine and dope

Which wont take you very far

Into the escape for which you hope

Yet you'll think as time goes on

That tho the last one didn't work

But then prehaps the next one may

Give you solace comfort hope

Once caressed and now you light

Causing near your face to gleam

A tiny bit of controlled fire

As into your face smoke stream

With a draw of clean breath you take

Deep into your mouth and lung

Polluted smoke to heat and cake

And destroy you from deep down

You who life did so much give

You who love so long has wooed

You who Earth and all that live

Waits for with hopes so high and proud

Into your new and tiny self

You again this demon draw

Here to slowly condemn yourself

By imitation of what you saw

Yes 'tis older ones they say

That has wisdom and is wise

But they too can lead astray

Earths true treasures Loves best prize

Just a little cigarette

Cannot much harm do you say

'Til you choke and pant for breath

And can no longer from them stay

Little girl or little boy

Take and aged fool's advice

Take your life live it enjoy

But avoid hate lust and vice

Do Not Bite Your Lovely Finger

Do not bite your lovely finger

As you sit and contemplate

Which card should now you render

To decide in this game your fate

Sit you on with pearl teeth gleaming

Parted slight by tempting tongue

Which vitalizes lips pulsating

As it wets lips and is gone

Now your fingers slowly creepeth

Resting on your forehead fair

Just above your hazel eyes

Just below your lovely hair

Both hands now face soft caressing

As you wait with face agleam

For the hand of cards you're pressing

As you scan them and you scheme

It is but a game you're playing

Only points to friendly end

Still you strive to keep from losing

Care not to win you do pretend

Alas life it is but a game too

But the stakes are different cast

We are dealt one hand to do

All life's game long as it may last

Pegging each mistake we fall back

Pegging every triumph go on

Try to reach first life's goal

Striving e'er to forward on

Stopping as life shows us reason

Whereby we may jump it seems

Contemplating mistakes to lessen

Losing points from life's lone dreams

You too are in life a player

Lovely tho you sit there now

You must play on too forever

So do not think so deeply now

Do not bite your lovely finger

Watch instead the sun and sea

Think of hope and love so tender

Leaving life's hard knocks for me

Bluer Than the Heavenly Sky

Bluer than the heavenly sky
Greener than grass with morning dew
Calmer than a new born child
Is the waters around this Isle
Whiter yet than fallen snow
Stretching before wherever you go
Besides the waters across the land
Is our soft virgin white coral sand
The trees upon the land do grow
With fruits you have and fruits you know
With many a strange fruit here and there
Mango, Paw-Paw, Sea grape and Avocado pear
It seems a shame to cut them down
To till our rich productive grounds
And more a shame to see them go
A big unmoral city there to grow
Our little cottages so neat and trim
Hold hospitality I'm told within
And these soon slum areas will be
If we allow outsiders to build their city
Our children's names are voiced far and near
Their decent discipline unfound visitors do declare
Across the world and thru the times
These people love and respect this land of mine
So how can we sit idly by

And see our fate like swallows fly
Across the sea with hardly a motion
But the majority die in the salty ocean
Our birds upon our trees do sing
Glad praises to our God and King
But how long will their song remain
If in a small cage they're kept in pain
Our fish quite free in the waters strive
Free food to keep the poor alive
But soon on our food will be a probation
If in quantities it's shipped to a foreign nation
Once you could drive quite economically
Now we must protect the third party
Our ways of transport must return to the horse and ass
As we see there's an increase in vehicle gas
How long how long will my people sit dumb
And take every decision of foreigners that come
And if someday our young rebel in hate
Wont it be because we acted too late
So let us try to do to them our duty
And come together in unbroken unity
Telling these fortune seekers quite frankly
We love their company but not their discriminality
This Isle with its waters trees and lovely sand
Is still our home Our Native Cayman
So why should it be us that is run out
"Freedom tho Poor" Caymanians let's hear the shout

A Wisp of a Dream

A wisp of a dream
In colour unfolds
Creating a vision for me
It shows there a picture
That to me is of old
Yet which haunts all of my memories
'Tis a vision of threads so soft
So silky so sweet so pure
That glitters and dances forever
Like new polished fresh spun gold
The gold is but the paint of nature
On the head of one dear to me
Which remains as a memory's picture
Which will always remain here with me
It comes and it softly lingers
In my dreams my mind and my life
Tho but a dream it ever will haunt me
Tho a vision it maketh my life
Yet who would be without dreams dear
Even tho they be fickle and few
We keep them and hope one day darling
That our most fickle ones will come true
So smile on you golden haired vision
Let your spun gold treads surround
The head that is holding these lips
Which kiss me while love doth abound
And as in your gold I do linger
As closer to me you I press
You know vision of gold I adore you
And long you once more to caress

<u>Worshipping Your Idols</u>

You've been worshipping your Idols

Made of silver and gold

Instead of worshipping the Saviour

The way you have been told

That's why your life can have no meaning

It's just hollow and cold

Cause you're worshipping your Idols

'Stead of making God your own

You can't deny that He gave you love

A love you never returned

You can't deny all the miseries of

The cross that He sojourned

You don't deserve no longer

The freedoms you have got

But He's still willing to forgive

'Cause you He loves a lot

Tak Me Hom Too De Wam Breeze

Tak me hom too de wam breeze

Let me wanda boat da n nite

Mong de cool singin willo trees

Swayin n de pale moonlite

Let me hare de watas wam

Lap on de wite san shorr

Wit a truu lov deep n me ams

Ah,ll be happe fa ewamorr

Let me njoy orr seasons all

As eac one com too pass

A twelwe mont suma, spring n fal

H a winta n a rom-filled glass

O gi me bak de homble spot

Way lik a chile a did plaa

Way de nite n da rr not too hot

N de temp in de sevente stay

Sho me gain dose open lans

Way at midnite a carrowsd

Lisenen too de sof calypso bans

Wich dancen riddem arowsd

Gi me bak de watas clare

Way orr frens on mene a nite

Had bech paties o rom n bare

Swimmen in de moonlite brite

Lisen too de natiws sing

N de free n opon waas

Tellen o lif, lov orr enyting

Bak frum day chilehood das

So tak me hom too de Ilan now

Put me on a Jet plene quik

All newa mor leav dere a wow

N mak meself homsik

Tak me tak me Tak me to me Ilan hom

Tak me Tak me Lawd a fe tiyad a room

Translation:

Take me home to the warm breeze

Let me wander both day and night

Among the cool singing willow trees

Swaying in the pale moonlight

Let me hear the waters warm

Lap on the white sands shore

With a true love deep in my arms

I'll be happy forevermore

Let me enjoy our seasons all

As each one comes to pass

A twelve month summer, spring and fall

An a winter in a rum-filled glass

Oh give me back the humble spot

Where as a child I played

Where the night and days are not too hot

An the temp in the seventies stay

Show me again those open lands

Where at midnight I caroused

Listening to the soft calypso bands

Which dancing rhythm aroused

Give me back the waters clear

Where our friends on many a night

Held beach parties of rum and beer

Swimming in the moonlight bright

Listen to the natives sing

In the free and open ways

Telling of life, love or anything

Back from their childhood days

So take me home to the Islands now

Put me on a jet plane quick

I'll nevermore leave there I vow

And make myself homesick

Take me take me take me to my Island home

Take me take me Lord I'm tired I roamed

I'm Just a Lonely Drifter

I'm just a lonely drifter
Like a log that's fallen wide
Away from boom secure
To drift on sea and tide
Lovers like ships they pass me
So silently they go
Without a word or smile or thought
Of the heartaches that I know
I drift on while the sea of time
Wash softly 'gainst my sides
In memories and deeper regrets
Of the days when love'd abide
No truth is left for me to seek
No life for me to live
Just a lonely drifter on the sea
Was the sentence life did give
I travel onwards ever on
'Til one day a love will stay
And place her arms around me warm
And drag me far away
The drifting logs all seem to wait
For the tug that pulls them in
So a lifetime drifter I'll remain
'Less you pull me out again
Yes I'm just a lonely drifter
Cast like logs on a moving tide
Away, away from booms secure
I drift the seas worldwide

Just Call to Me My Darling

Just call to me my Darling

Whenever you're afraid

Tho there's not much which I have

To offer but myself

Yet I'll give that my Darling

To do with as you will

If in return one day I'd learn

That my wrong you did forgive

I had your love so sacred

A lasting warmth and joy

But being only Human

I acted like a boy

Now she is gone away dear

Yes the child she lost was mine

And tho I loved that child too dear

It's for you my heart still pines

I know it's hard to take now

And live with all you life

But I am still your husband,

You are still my wife

I can only ask your pardon
For the wrong that I have done
And that you'd take me back again
To be a father to my son

Our daughter small and tiny
If I should stay away
Would never really miss me
'Cept at home at work at play
But little crippled Jimmy
Will beg and be so sad
Each time he looks for comfort
And cannot find his Dad

So take this humble prayer dear
As it comes deep from my heart
In deep regret yet quite sincere
And hopeful to the last
Here among the wayward fathers
Is where I can be found
Should you ever find it in your heart
To forgive the one who let you down

I'm Asking Your Forgiveness

I'm asking your forgiveness
For I have done you wrong
I've been around another
I know I've put you down
You'll never understand dear
Just what you meant to me
But now you're brokenhearted
You ask to be set free

You ask dear for your freedom
You ask that I say yes
You ask it tho you know dear
I could never love you less
You are to me my heaven
My earth and life and love
You're my eternal promise
Of a future life above

So tho I've hurt you deeply
In my hasty senseless way
I'll love you still forever
As I've loved you yesterday
So take my hand and hold it
Let me press you to my heart
There to love you dear forever
In life and soul and heart

Today I Cried For You

Today I cried for you

Knowing of the sadness you've been through

The hurts and aches

The pains you've felt

And how you too must have ached for help and knelt

The agony of being lonely

And so alone

The sweetness of love

And the cruel hate you've known

But from this cold and strife

There must be a better life

Just like from long falling rain

The rainbow brings the sun again

Soon there'll dawn a brighter day

No more will there be a burden to pay

All will be happy and oh so gay

Like the growing flowers in the month of May

No more to care what people say

The dawning of that suns ray

Will show alas — the glistening way

Blue Blue Blue

Blue --------

Blue ----------------

Blue ------------------------

The beauty of the never-ending blue

From reaches of the dusty clouds

That ring the far horizon

To brightness of the noontime bright

The splendour seems to've risen

From powder to the deep azure

From Turquoise thru to Royal

From faint and plain

To loud and full

You show your everlasting beauty

Blue --------

Blue ----------------

Blue ------------------------

Tho clouds they try to hide you

Tho Suns bright light doth come

Seems it only comes to serve you

Tho far beyond and far above

We've tried and tried to reach

You stay so far in hidden love

To hold our awe and teach

Your beauty it in unsurpassed

Your lasting radiance glimmers

As you do span our Universe

And all of your blue shades fill us

So Blue, Blue, Blue

Stay near where you belong

And Blue, Blue, Blue

We'll praise you e'er in song

I Believe in Christmas

I believe in Christmas
More at Christmas time each year
As I listen to the songs they sing
Which tell of Christmas cheer.
I believe in Christmas
The birthday of our Lord
And join in celebration full
The season's fun and its accord.
I believe in Christmas
Each time a flake I see
Of soft pure first winters snow
A-glistening on the tree.
I believe in Christmas
In Christmas simple and so pure
Wherein we all are friends of man
Old or young the rich and poor.
I believe in Christmas
But not all of this glitter
Which lines the stores to draw you in
While carols softly twitter.
I believe in Christmas
But it brings my heart to shame
At all the commerce it creates
While forgetting full His name.
I believe in Christmas
I believe in what its worth
Thru love and joy and sharing
With others here on Earth.
Yes I believe in Christmas
And I hope that yours be grand
As you enjoy it as he would
Thankful of Gods gift to man.

So This Is Christmas... Is It?

So this is Christmas... is it?

If I a stranger to this time

If I a stranger to this land

Had followed course and wandered

Like pilgrim old from foreign shore

It yet would be November

The feathers warm yet from the bird

Which graced our dinner table

Would but signal me Thanksgiving

For bounteous harvest barely o'er

'Fore the long cold days of winter

And I would ne'er have given thought

To Yuletimes' gloss and glitter.

So this is Christmas... is it?

The time to recollect again

The time to ponder on the birth

Of one known as the son of men

He lay they say upon the straw

In open cattle manger

With naught but cows and sheep

Goats, camels and shepherd stranger

Their groans and grunts and bleats
Their nasal welcome song
As this the Yuletime's reason
This son of God 'twas born.

So this is Christmas... is it?
Love laughter joy and peace
Hope help and outward giving
That receive now some will each
Where to give is now a pleasure
Returns thought not of you say
The spirit full of peace on earth
Goodwill to all on Christmas Day
So this is Christmas... is it?
Nay hypocrite and liar
'Tis but another rouse you use
To get what you desire.

So this is Christmas... is it?
Which starts three fortnights back
To help those who would profit here
Set up full their hype attack
Tinsel and the sounds of songs
Not heard throughout the year

Mixed with the helpful "gimme" calls
Of bells chimes loud and clear
The sale of sales in every store
To psyche out the hardest heart
Combined with tele's touching shows
Of how the goodwill starts
All interspersed with "buy this" shots
So well perfected is the art.

So this is Christmas... is it?
The hard and soft sales pitch
The enticement for the young ones
Unaware of the costs of it
The shiny tinsel red and green
To capture hearts imagination
So thoughtlessly commercials flash
Uncaring of the debts situation
The haves a Christmas time will know
Such as the havenots of but dream
But this is what the sales pitch says
In red debt or in cash green
In songs that tell the little ones
Who yet to read cannot
Of dolls and wagons, gifts and toys

Which from Santa must be sought
Of but two ways he they will judge
When the time of joy rolls 'round
The bad will be those left without
While the good with gifts abound.

So this is Christmas... is it?
When peace should shine on earth
When son of man remembered is
Who was poor thru life from birth
Then tell me now a stranger here
As your stores flash out their wares
Where hides this goodwill of yours
Thruout all of the year
Where does the poor and lonely child
Find the Santa's you portray
When his daily bread but scarcely sent
Is from his begging day to day
Where does the orphan or outcast
Find a toy a doll or gift
When freezing on snow-covered roads
You refuse them in your car a lift
What good is being good each year
Brought when there at years end

That visioned judge 'Old Santa Claus'

Rejects those poor again

Is then not bad at Christmas-time

Like thruout all of the year

But judged in full by dollars held

Instead of the good you share

And like the justice which law affords

To those who for it can pay

So too the richer boy and girl

Is the good child on Christmas Day.

So this is Christmas... is it?

If it is and you say it holds

Then enjoy your glint and glitter

And all it will you afford

For to me you've lost the meaning

Of a poor and humble birth

Encased in foil and gold and song

In a hyped commercial earth

You've failed to see the want and pain

Which your ways has caused to man

You've failed to dry the children's eyes

Who stand alone with empty hand

Yes if this is Christmas... keep it

I a stranger thru has passed

To be bewildered and dumbstruck

By all things you have amassed

The gifts, the toys, the soft sell

The songs which praise the day

Six weeks before its coming

You herald in its stay

Yet your Christmas time is empty

Your blazing fire's not warm

'Til you recall in full the truth

Why Christ on this earth was born

So hang you hollow gloss and glitter

From store and home and street

Wish you meaningless "Merry Christmas"

To shoppers fortunate you'll meet

Go and see your fake 'Santa Claus'

Thrill you with things to buy

Close once again your eyes to the poor

As you silently pass them by....

So this is Christmas... is it?

Is it?

Is it?

Late Tonight

Late tonight when the music is gone

Late tonight when we've both gone on home

There in the darkness of night I will see

Your face as it comes back to me

Again your face will slowly appear

Once more you in memory'll be there

Then I'll know you as I did before

As we walk in memories once more

Not oft do I see a face that'll stay

Not oft do I forget one 'long the way

And as yours I'm certain before I beheld

That's why in my thoughts deeply you dwell

Where was it and when I do not recall

How it happened I'm not sure of at all

Yet engraved for some reason you remain

Your face form and figure exactly the same

No error I make in my recognition

Only dimmed thought of place and situation

So 'til in my dreams tonight you I see

I'll wonder til you return in my Memories

It's Been Nice

It's been nice to pay a visit
To the olden times I've known
To speak again with old warm friends
Made fast in days now gone
To see the faces new that be
To hear their happy chatter
Once more recall the fleeting past
Where I've spent such happy hours
Yet I can see the old days too
When alone I'd sit and think
'Tis funny that these too come back
Whene'er of the past I think
Not much has changed
Except prehaps a face, a name
A position or a body
Yet even all the new it seems
The same one like the other
And so life goes from year to year
As time and friendships fly
One day to meet and greet hello
One day short and then goodbye
So friend old and acquaintance new
As we say this time adieu
I'll keep e'er warm in memory
This pleasant time spent again with you

Heaven Earth and Tearful Heart

Heaven Earth and tearful heart e'er responding
Hell eternal always trying hard empty remains
So life stands and so love has beginnings
So dreams are borne and so hope finds an end
What then remains for man to look up to
What pinnacle wherefrom they'll no longer fall
Alas 'tis but belief and trust unending
And desires from which there's no respite at all
What then my heart I cry to visions clouded
Why hope you yet to reach for yonder peak
Ah but too near that vision
Be my heart's respondings
Brings joy and life anew to hear her speak
Oh Hell eternal at thy hearth eyes reaching
Like the hands of a drowning man outstretch
Oh Heaven Earth and tired Heart endlessly roving
Seek love, life, warmth and contentment
For this wretch
But now in jest you gaze and you do wonder
If it's but a new toy here again that you've found
You think to care but carefully you ponder
To keep it safe or alas to cast it down
So life once more holds days of full laughter
Joyous nights so near yet so apart
Loving to be just within sight of each other
Sharing the sweet silent language of the heart
Oh Heaven and Earth alas this hearts end runneth
Without a thought or worry or a care
For all Hells endings and the Heavens
Eternal rulings
Can ne'er again change our short moments shared

Table of Contents Poem

As I had related in my foreword to 'Dear Reader,' that one could almost take the Table of Contents list and read it as a poem of itself. For me, this is what comes to mind:

Tides Ebb And Flow ~ *around our feet*

Here We Sit Talking ~ *just me and my*

Beautiful Persistent Sunworshipper

While I'm Writing To You Dear Mom

My Prayers Are Answered...

As A Woman ~ *approaches*

Only A Picture ~ *or mayhap a dream to*

Brighten Some Corner ~ *of my lonely life*

Beautiful Eyes So Softly ~ *calling and capturing*

I Was Just A Blackbird ~ *watching life go by*

There Are But Two People ~ *two souls so alone*

Oh So Dark And Dismal Grey...

The Weatherman Today Says Rain ~ *again*

I Saw The Big Big Fair City ~ *all around me loudly*

My Colours They Have Always Been ~ *green, gold and blue*

Gee But It's Calm And Peaceful ~ *as I recall hot tropics*

A Bright And Sunny Day...

You Cold White Soft Demon ~ *called snow*

Old Seven Mile Stretch ~ *can never relate to you*

Silver Dollars All Aglitter ~ *snowflakes in the air*

Let Me Sail All My Days Away ~ *as tides ebb and flow*

Alas Darling I'm Only A Dreamer ~ *a life and love seeker*

'Twas The Night Before Full Moon ~ *as I gaze into the sky*

Just Like Liquid Glass It Lies ~ *this bit of ancient ocean shore*

Spotted Jagged Treed Or Bare ~ *reflecting to my mind*

'Tis But A Tiny Bit Of Weed ~ *but, we flip it away unwanted*

Do Not Bite Your Lovely Finger ~ *as you deeply contemplate*

Bluer Than The Heavenly Sky ~ *your eyes a sparkle throws*

A Wisp Of A Dream ~ *long past, but hopefully to reappear*

Worshipping Your Idols ~ *or trinkets or possessions*

Tak Me Hom Too De Wam Breeze ~ *an islands accent*

I'm Just A Lonely Drifter ~ *maybe a lot like you*

Just Call To Me My Darling ~ *call me if you ever I you need*

I'm Asking Your Forgiveness ~ *for even once making you grieve*

Today I Cried For You ~ *alone, lost and drifting apart*

Blue Blue Blue ~ *blue blue blue*

I Believe In Christmas ~ *yes I do! I hope you do too*

So This Is Christmas... Is It? ~ *it could be if I could see you*

Late Tonight ~ *for just a moment to hold onto*

It's Been Nice ~ *it's been nice, it's been so so nice*

Heaven Earth & Tearful Heart ~ *e'er rejoicing calling out your name*

Other Collections by This Author:

www.ingramcontent.com/pod-product-compliance
Lightning Source LLC
Chambersburg PA
CBHW032106080426
42733CB00006B/449